RHYME TIME

OXFORD
UNIVERSITY PRESS

Great Clarendon Street, Oxford OX2 6DP
Oxford University Press is a department of the University of Oxford.
It furthers the University's objective of excellence in research, scholarship,
and education by publishing worldwide in

Oxford   New York
Athens   Auckland   Bangkok   Bogotá   Buenos Aires
Calcutta   Cape Town   Chennai   Dar es Salaam   Delhi
Florence   Hong Kong   Istanbul   Karachi   Kuala Lumpur
Madrid   Melbourne   Mexico City   Mumbai   Nairobi   Paris
São Paulo   Singapore   Taipei   Tokyo   Toronto   Warsaw

with associated companies in   Berlin   Ibadan

Oxford is a registered trade mark of Oxford University Press
in the UK and in certain other countries

British Library Cataloguing in Publication Data available

ISBN 0 19 276227 3 (hardback)
ISBN 0 19 276228 1 (paperback)

Typeset by Sarah Nicholson
Printed in Malaysia

RHYME TIME

Around the day

Compiled by JOHN FOSTER

Illustrated by CAROL THOMPSON

OXFORD
UNIVERSITY PRESS

Acknowledgements

We are grateful to the authors for permission to include the following poems, all of which are published for the first time in this collection.

Jane Clarke: 'Book Shop', copyright © Jane Clarke 2000; **Lucy Coats:** 'Fast Asleep in Africa', copyright © Lucy Coats 2000; **Andrew Collett:** 'Good Morning, Toys!' and 'Bedtime Counting' both copyright © Andrew Collett 2000; **Paul Cookson:** 'Just One More', copyright © Paul Cookson 2000; **Wendy Cope:** 'Talking', copyright © Wendy Cope 2000; **Sue Cowling:** 'Little Red Van' and 'Going Shopping', both copyright © 2000; **Lynette Craig:** 'Bedtime', copyright © Lynette Graham 2000; **Eric Finney:** 'What's in the Dark?', copyright © Eric Finney 2000; **John Foster:** 'The Morning Rush' copyright © John Foster 2000; **Carolyn Graham:** 'Scrambled Eggs', copyright © Carolyn Graham 2000; **Nigel Gray:** 'Playschool', copyright © Nigel Gray 2000; **Maureen Haselhurst:** 'Something in the Bath', copyright © Maureen Haselhurst 2000; **Mike Johnson:** 'Paintbox', copyright © Mike Johnson 2000; **Jean Kenward:** 'The Shop', copyright © Jean Kenward 2000; **John Kitching:** 'Tale Time', copyright © John Kitching 2000; **Tony Langham:** 'Chips' and 'Bedtime Song', both copyright © Tony Langham 2000; **Patricia Leighton:** 'Playschool Favourites', copyright © Patricia Leighton 2000; **Wes Magee:** 'Dressing-up', 'Action Rhyme Time', and 'In the Supermarket' all copyright © Wes Magee 2000; **Ian McMillan:** 'Sock Song' copyright © Ian McMillan 2000; **Tony Mitton:** 'Here Comes the Postman', 'Bedmates', and 'The Corner Shop' all copyright Tony Mitton 2000; **Barbara Moore:** 'Soup', copyright © Barbara Moore 2000; **Judith Nicholls:** 'Finger Painting', copyright © Judith Nicholls; **Cynthia Rider:** 'Exercise Time' and 'Bubble-Bath', both copyright © Cynthia Rider 2000; **Coral Rumble:** 'Today I'll Be A Knight' copyright © Coral Rumble 2000; **Matt Simpson:** 'Beddy-Byes', copyright © Matt Simpson 2000; **Marian Swinger:** 'Sleepyhead', copyright © Marian Swinger 2000; **Jill Townsend:** 'Mess', copyright © Jill Townsend 2000; **Clive Webster:** 'My Birthday Party', copyright © Clive Webster 2000; **David Whitehead:** 'Belinda', copyright © David Whitehead 2000.

We also acknowledge permission to include previously published poems:

Gina Douthwaite: 'Sammy Somersault' from *Picture a Poem* (Hutchinson, 1994), copyright © Gina Douthwaite 1994, reprinted by permission of the author; **Linda Hammond:** 'Pancakes' from *Five Furry Teddy Bears* (Penguin, 1990), copyright © Linda Hammond 1990, reprinted by permission of Penguin Books Ltd; **Shirley Hughes:** 'Squirting Rainbows' from *Out and About* (Walker Books, 1988), © Shirley Hughes 1988, reprinted by permission of the publisher; **Michelle Magorian:** 'Cakes' from *Orange Paw Marks* (Viking Books, 1989), copyright © Michelle Magorian 1989, reprinted by permission of the author c/o Rogers, Coleridge and White Ltd, 20 Powis Mews, London, W11 1JN; **Tony Mitton:** 'Towers', first published in *Early Years Poems & Rhymes* compiled by Jill Bennett (Scholastic, 1993), reprinted by permission of the author; **Judith Nicholls:** 'Sounds Good' from *Higgledy Humbug* (Mary Glasgow Publications, 1990), copyright © Judith Nicholls 1990, reprinted by permission of the author; **Joan Poulson:** 'Like an Animal', copyright © Joan Poulson 1991, first published in *Twinkle, Twinkle Chocolate Bar* compiled by John Foster (OUP, 1991), reprinted by permission of the author; **Coral Rumble:** 'Toothpaste Trouble', copyright © Coral Rumble 1999, first published in *Hop to the Sky* compiled by Brian Moses, (Ginn, 1999), reprinted by permission of the author; **John Smith:** 'Mud' from *The Early Bird* (Burke Books).

Although we have tried to trace and contact copyright holders before publication, in one or two cases this has not been possible. If contacted we will be pleased to rectify the omission and any errors at the earliest opportunity.

Contents

Time To Get Up

Time For School

Time For Shopping

Time For Play

Time For Tea

Time For Bed

--- • ---

Time To Get Up

--- • ---

Sleepyhead

Wake up, wake up, you sleepyhead,
Teddy's fallen out of bed,
birds are singing in the trees,
washing's blowing in the breeze,
the postman's been, the sun's come out,
the milk's arrived, so let's all shout,
'WAKE UP, WAKE UP, YOU SLEEPYHEAD,
IT'S MUCH TOO LATE TO BE IN BED!'

Marian Swinger

Good Morning, Toys!

First a rustle then a rumble
a shudder and a shake,
as, early in the morning,
my toys start to wake.

They always get up early
it's always been this way,
for the earlier they wake up
the sooner they can play.

Andrew Collett

9

Sammy Somersault

When Sammy Somersault awoke
he tippletailed before he spoke.
He did three backward flips into
his jumper, trousers, and one shoe
then tied his lace in lots of bows
while balancing upon his nose.
Sam cartwheeled, stood upon his head
then, almost dressed, bounced back to bed.

Gina Douthwaite

Sock Song

Upstairs
Downstairs
Where can they be?
I can't find my socks
and they can't find me!

Bedroom
Bathroom
Where have they gone?
I can't find my socks
and I need to put them on!

Inside
Outside
Hanging on the line?
I can't find my socks
and I'm running out of time!

One sock
Two socks
Silly things to lose
and when I've found my socks…

I'll be hunting for my shoes!

Ian McMillan

11

Fast Asleep in Africa

Fast asleep in Africa
Waking up in France
Getting up each morning
Is a time to sing and dance.

Waffles in the garden
Fried eggs by the sea
Cornflakes in the kitchen
Smells like breakfast time to me.

Lucy Coats

Here Comes the Postman

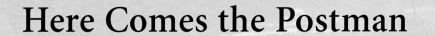

Here comes the postman
dressed in blue.
Will there be a letter
for me or you?

Quick! Look!
He's stopping at our gate.
What has he got for us?
I just can't wait.

Here comes a letter
slipping through our door.
Let's go and pick it up
and find out who it's for.

Tony Mitton

The Morning Rush

Into the bathroom,
Turn on the tap.
Wash away the sleepiness —
Splish! Splosh! Splash!

Into the bedroom,
Pull on your vest.
Quickly! Quickly!
Get yourself dressed.

Down to the kitchen.
No time to lose.
Gobble up your breakfast.
Put on your shoes.

14

Back to the bathroom.
Squeeze out the paste.
Brush, brush, brush your teeth.
No time to waste.

Look in the mirror.
Comb your hair.
Hurry, scurry, hurry, scurry
Down the stairs.

Pick your school bag
Up off the floor.
Grab your coat.
And out through the door.

John Foster

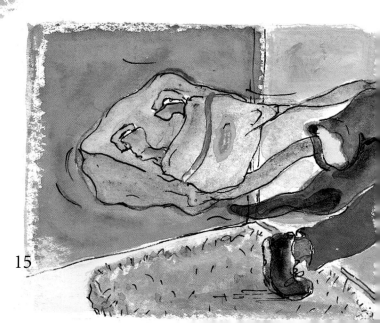

Scrambled Eggs

Scrambled eggs, milk, and honey
I'm having breakfast
with the Easter Bunny!

Scrambled eggs, pancakes too
I'm having breakfast
with a kangaroo

Scrambled eggs, jelly on a spoon
I'm having breakfast
with the Man in the Moon

Porridge, pancakes, apple cider
I'm having breakfast
with the itsy-bitsy spider

Poached eggs, fried eggs, bacon, ham
I'm having breakfast
with Mary's little lamb

Hey, little doggie, clap your paws
We're having breakfast
with Santa Claus!

Carolyn Graham

Time For School

Playschool

I like doing puzzles,
and playing with toys,
and building with bricks,
and chasing the boys.

I like dressing up,
and making a band,
and splashing in water,
and digging in sand.

I like the tunnel,
and the climbing frame.
And knocking down skittles
is a really good game.

I like cutting out,
and playing with clay,
and finger-painting,
and the 'Interest Tray'.

I like blowing bubbles,
and the bikes we ride,
and the big see-saw,
and the slippery slide.

I like singing a song,
and chanting a rhyme,
and tidying up,
and story time.

I like seeing friends,
and the games we play,
It's fun at Playschool
every day.

Nigel Gray

19

Dressing-Up

You can be a Pirate,
I will be a Clown,
and Ben can be the Postman
walking round the town.

You can be a Princess,
I will be a Knight,
and Faye can be a Monster
and give us all a fright.

You can be a Spaceman,
I will be the Queen,
and Jack can be a Giant
dressed in red and green.

You can be a Cowboy,
I will be a King,
and Dean can be a Wizard
with a magic ring.

You can be a Doctor,
I will be the Nurse,
and Jo can be our Teacher
reading us this verse.

Wes Magee

Action Rhyme Time

You're a hedgehog
rolled in a ball.

You're a horse
jumping a wall.

You're a mouse
nibbling at cheese.

You're a dog
scratching its fleas.

You're a hen
pecking at straw

And you're a cat
asleep on the floor.

Wes Magee

Paintbox

Can't find blue,
but here is green.
The strangest coloured
sky I've seen.

Can't find yellow,
but here is white.
My brilliant sun's
a lovely sight.

Can't find brown,
but here is red.
I'll have to use
this shade, instead.

There, I've finished.
Come and see!
Green sky, white sun
and bright red me.

Mike Johnson

22

Finger Painting

Dip your finger,
dip your thumb
Dip and drip,
drip and dip;

nearly done!

Finger red,
yellow thumb

press and mix
colour tricks,

See that sun!

Judith Nicholls

Playschool Favourites

I love it in the sandpit
And on the climbing frame.
I love slip-slopping paint around
And playing 'chase me' games.

I love it in the water corner
SPLISH—SPLASH—SPLOSH
But best of all is when we stop
For biscuits and squash!

Patricia Leighton

Exercise Time

I can do a roly-poly
I can hop on the spot
I can swing like a monkey
I can gallop and trot.

I can leapfrog over Jack
I can bounce like a ball
But when I balance on the bar
I wobble off…and fall!

Cynthia Rider

Tale Time

Tales about pigs,
Tales about goats,
Tales about trolls,
Tales about boats.

Tales about fairies,
Tales about mice,
Tales about giants
And sugar and spice.

Tales about beanstalks,
Tales about kings,
Tales about ghosts
And magical rings.

I love going to school,
All the work and the play,
But, best, I love story
At end of the day!

John Kitching

Time For Shopping

The Shop

We must hurry
  we must hurry
    to the Supermarket
    Shop,
for it's raining —
  yes, it's raining —
    and it isn't going
    to stop,

And I'm splashing
  in the puddles
    just as everybody
    should,
and our baby's
  in the buggy
    with a funny, plastic
    hood.

We must hurry
  we must hurry
    to the Supermarket
    Shop
where it's warm and dry
  and out of all
    the plipple
      and the plop.

We'll fold up our
  umbrellas
    till they're straight, and thin
    and small,
and you'll never guess
  there'd ever been
    a rainy day
    at all!

Jean Kenward

In the Supermarket Trolley

Mum puts us in the trolley,
  Baby Joe and me.
She piles the food around us
  — carrots, milk, and tea.
Up and down the aisles we go.
  Lots of things to see.
The man at check-out hands
  a lollipop to me.
And now we're heading for the car.
  Faster, Mum!
    Wow-Weeeeeeeeeeeeeee!

Wes Magee

Going Shopping

Don't want to try it on!
Don't need a dress!
You must know how big I am —
Can't you just guess?

Don't want to try them on!
Don't like new shoes!
You must know what size I am —
Why don't you choose?

Sue Cowling

Talking

When we go out for a walk
And Mummy meets a friend,
They stop and talk and talk and talk
And drive me round the bend.

Talking, talking, talking.
Such a lot to say.
Grown-ups! Always talking.
Don't they want to play?

I'm tired of standing quietly.
It's boring here, you know.
Everyone's ignoring me.
Come on. I want to go.

Talking, talking, talking.
Such a lot to say.
Grown-ups! Always talking.
Don't they want to play?

Wendy Cope

Little Red Van

Mum, can I have a ride?
It's only 30p.
I can drive the little red van
And you can wave to me.

Dad, can I have a ride?
It's two for 50p.
I can sing the postman's song
And you can sing with me.

Nan, can I have a ride?
It's five goes for a pound.
You come too and be the cat
That helps me do my round!

Sue Cowling

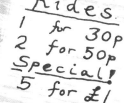

Rides.
1 for 30p
2 for 50p
Special!
5 for £1

The Corner Shop

Let's go down to the corner shop.
It's full of lots of things.
There's tubs of sweets
and chocolate treats
and shiny silver rings.

There's Little Pony rubbers
and stickers that look like stars.
There's tiny trains and plastic planes
and crayons just like cars.

Let's go down to the corner shop.
I've got 50p.
So can we go?
Because I know
there's something there for me.

Tony Mitton

Book Shop

So much to choose from! So many books!
Let's take our time and sit down and look.
Books about princesses and witches and fairies,
Books about monsters and other hairy scaries.
Pop-up books to make you laugh,
Waterproof books to take in the bath.
Books about making things, and things to do.
Books about visits to the farm and the zoo.
Books about animals and insects and birds.
Books full of pictures. Books full of words.
So much to choose from. Let's take our time.
How about this one? A book full of rhymes.

Jane Clarke

Time For Play

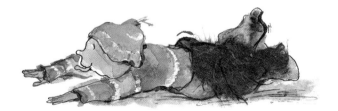

Belinda

Belinda, Belinda,
　Now, dry your sad eyes.
The rain has stopped falling,
　The sun climbs the skies.
The tears on your window
　Will soon fade away.
The children are calling

Belinda!
　　　　　Let's play!

Oh! Belinda, Belinda,
　Didn't you know?
There have to be showers
　For flowers to grow.
Look! Here comes the sunshine,
　The rain clouds have gone.
The children are calling

Belinda!
　　　　　Come on!

David Whitehead

Squirting Rainbows

Bare legs,
Bare toes,
Paddling pool,
Garden hose.
Daisies sprinkled
In the grass,
Dandelions
Bold as brass.
Squirting rainbows,
Sunbeam flashes,
Backyards full
Of shrieks and splashes!

Shirley Hughes

Like an Animal

I snarl and snap
around the park
pretend that I'm a
strong fierce shark

I jump and hop
off a fallen log
pretend that I'm a
bright-eyed frog.

I slide zigzag
beside the lake
pretend that I'm a
patterned snake

I leap and spring
bound everywhere
pretend that I'm a
long-legged hare

Joan Poulson

38

Mud

I like mud.
  I like it on my clothes.
I like it on my fingers.
  I like it on my toes.

Dirt's pretty ordinary
  And dust's a dud.
For a really good mess-up
  I like mud.

John Smith

39

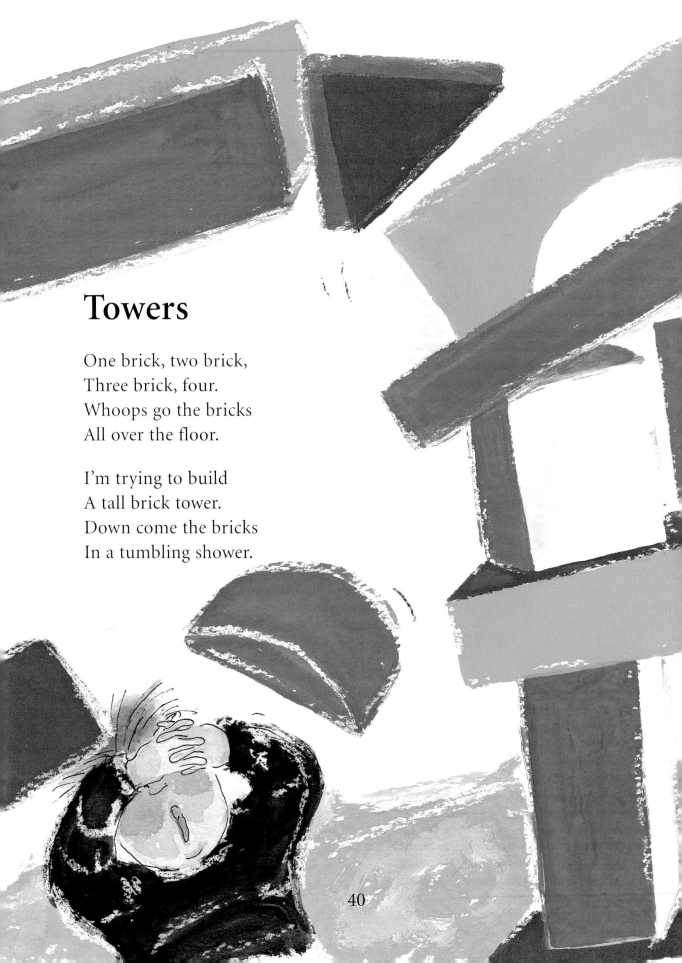

Towers

One brick, two brick,
Three brick, four.
Whoops go the bricks
All over the floor.

I'm trying to build
A tall brick tower.
Down come the bricks
In a tumbling shower.

Balance one, perch one…
A trembling stack.
Smash, bang, clatter,
Smackety crack.

Here's another tower.
Watch it sway.
Here comes a hand
To knock it away.

Tony Mitton

41

Today I'll Be A Knight

Today I think I'll be a knight
With a saucepan on my head,
I'll ride a horse around the house,
Well, perhaps a broom instead.

I'll slay a dragon on the stairs
Who looks just like our cat,
Before I fight a wicked king
Who's as floppy as our mat.

Then I'll climb a towering wall,
There will be no stopping me,
Unless I hear my mum call out,
'Come down, it's time for tea!'

Coral Rumble

· —————— · ——————

Time For Tea

· —————— · ——————

Sounds Good

Sausage sizzles,
crispbreads crack;
hot dogs hiss
and flapjacks snap!

Bacon boils
and fritters fry;
apples squelch
in apple pie.

Baked beans bubble,
gravy grumbles;
popcorn pops,
and stomach rumbles…

I'M HUNGRY!

Judith Nicholls

Chips

I like sausages
I like eggs
I like fish fingers
and chicken legs —
they all slide easily
past my lips
but most of all
I LOVE CHIPS!

I like spaghetti
I like beans
I like pizza
and soggy greens —
they all slide easily
past my lips
but most of all
I LOVE CHIPS!

I like cornflakes
I like toast
I like gravy
on a Sunday roast —
they all slide easily
past my lips
but most of all
I LOVE CHIPS!!!

Tony Langham

45

My Birthday Party

Today's my birthday party,
It starts at half past three,
And all my friends are coming
To play and have their tea.

Mummy's made a birthday cake
With icing sweet and pink.
There's sausage rolls and
   sandwiches,
And lemonade to drink.

We'll all play 'pass the parcel'
To find what's wrapped inside,
And next a game that's called
   'sardines' —
I wonder where I'll hide.

And when the party's over
There's one thing left to do —
Say 'Thank you all for coming,
And for your presents too!'

Clive Webster

Cakes

A cake filled with jam,
A cake filled with cream,
A cake decorated
With an iced football team.

A cake with chocolate,
A cake light as air,
A cake like a railway train,
A cake cut square,

Small cakes with cherries,
Large cakes with flags,
Long cakes and tall cakes,
Stale cakes in bags.

Cakes in the window
For someone to eat,
Just the thing
For a tea-time treat.

Michelle Magorian

47

Pancakes

Pancakes, pancakes, pancakes for tea.
Who'd like to make some pancakes with me?
We'll mix them and beat them
And toss them once more.
Oh no! Mine's just landed
Face down on the floor!

Linda Hammond

Soup

Soup, soup, glorious soup,
Soup that goes 'SLURP'
And soup that goes 'GLOOP'.
Soup that is thick,
And soup that is thin,
And soup that goes dribbling
All down your chin!

Barbara Moore

Mess

Gravy on the table.
Pudding in my hair.
A spoonful of custard
can go anywhere!
Mum says eat more slowly,
blow gently on hot food.
Eating too quickly
is really rather rude.
But, Mum, I'm hungry.
I've been at school all day.
Soon it'll be bedtime.
I need time left to play.

Jill Townsend

— • —

Time For Bed

— • —

Bedtime

Five more minutes — PLEASE
Five more minutes
I don't want to go to bed.

Oh, just five more minutes, please
Can't I stay here instead?

I promise I'll be very quiet
I've been so good all day —

Five more minutes, please
To stay downstairs and play.

Lynette Craig

Just One More…

Just one more drink, I promise…
Just one more biscuit then…
Just one more cuddle and I will
Go upstairs again…

Just one more goodnight kiss
Just one more video
Just one more story, maybe two
And then to bed I'll go…

CLEAN YOUR TEETH!
GO TO THE LOO!
GET TO BED!
I'M TELLING YOU!
DO IT NOW
YOU'LL GET WHAT FOR…

Mu-um, Da-ad…just one more…

Paul Cookson

Bubble-Bath

Bubbles here
Bubbles there
Clouds of bubbles
Everywhere.

On my tummy
On my toes
In my ears
And up my nose.

On my chin
And in my hair
Clouds of bubbles
Everywhere.

Cynthia Rider

Something in the Bath!

Something's hiding in the bubbles.
Something's sneaking round the plug.
Something's underneath the face cloth.
Something's by the toothbrush mug.
It bobs down by the hot tap
Then suddenly it sinks.
It doesn't look too scary
It's cute and round and pink.
I'm going to biff it with my sponge!
That Something has to go…

BIFF! SPLASH! OUCH! OW!

Why didn't someone tell me
That Something was MY TOE!

Maureen Haselhurst

Toothpaste Trouble

I can use the flannel,
I can use the soap,
But when I use the toothpaste
I give up all hope.

I get
Toothpaste on my cheek,
Toothpaste on my nose,
Toothpaste on my ear,
Toothpaste on my clothes.
Toothpaste on my tummy,
Toothpaste on my knee,
And in lots of other places
That toothpaste shouldn't be!

Coral Rumble

Beddy-Byes

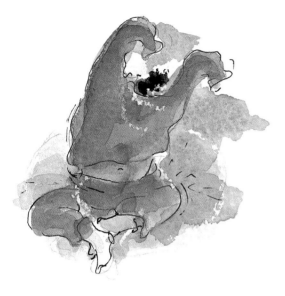

Scrub your teeth,
scrub your teeth,
scrub them shiny white!
Slip on your jim-jams,
Say Goodnight.

Rub your eyes,
rub your eyes!
Aren't you feeling dozy?
Here's a hot water bottle
to help you feel more
    cosy!

Head upon the pillow —
what's a pillow for?
Snuggle up with Teddy,
SNORE, SNORE,
    SNORE!!!!

Matt Simpson

Bedtime Counting

One is the moon shining on high

Two are the stars shooting through sky,

Three are the socks under my bed

Four are the pillows wrapped round my head,

Five are the toys left on the floor

And six are the kisses Dad blows through my door.

Andrew Collett

Bedmates

When it's time for bed I stumble
slowly up the stairs.
I take my dolly and my book
and both my little bears.

We snuggle up together
as I read us all a story,
until my dolly starts to yawn
and both my bears are snorey.

Then I put the book aside
and tuck us all in tight.
And off we drift together
on the dreamy tide of night.

Tony Mitton

What's in the Dark?

What's in the dark,
When goodnights have been said
And the lights are turned out
And I'm here in my bed?
There are voices downstairs —
Mum and Dad's quiet chat;
I can't tell what they're saying
But I don't mind that;
Footsteps down in the street,
In the distance a train,
Car lights in my window,
It's starting to rain.
There's a rumble from somewhere
A long way away:
Big lorries perhaps
On the motorway.
And I'm warm in the dark
And I think as I lie
Of my favourite books
And my toys just close by.
Now I'm dozy, I'm dreamy,
I'm nearly away…
And out of the dark
Will come dawn and the day.

Eric Finney

Bedtime Song

Sleepy-head, sleepy-head
Time to find your way to bed

And snuggle down with your teddy
Or favourite doll, they're always ready

To cuddle close through the night
Sleeping till the morning light

Comes again to start the day
And you can play and play and play

Until once more your sleepy-head
Tells you that it's time for bed.

Tony Langham

Index of Titles and First Lines
First lines are in italics

Index of Authors